LIVING WITH
AUTISM

ABDO
Publishing Company

LIVING WITH AUTISM

by Megan Atwood

Content Consultant

Dr. Sandra Harris, PhD, Board of Governors Distinguished
Service Professor Emerita, Rutgers University, New Brunswick, NJ

LIVING WITH HEALTH CHALLENGES

CREDITS

Published by ABDO Publishing Company, PO Box 398166, Minneapolis, MN 55439. Copyright © 2012 by Abdo Consulting Group, Inc. International copyrights reserved in all countries. No part of this book may be reproduced in any form without written permission from the publisher. The Essential Library™ is a trademark and logo of ABDO Publishing Company.

Printed in the United States of America,
North Mankato, Minnesota
102011
012012

 THIS BOOK CONTAINS AT LEAST 10% RECYCLED MATERIALS.

Contributing Author: Beth A. Glasberg
Editor: Lisa Owings
Copy Editor: Jessica Hillstrom
Series design and cover production: Becky Daum
Interior production: Kazuko Collins

Library of Congress Cataloging-in-Publication Data
Atwood, Megan.
  Living with autism / by Megan Atwood.
     p. cm. -- (Living with health challenges)
   ISBN 978-1-61783-123-2
  1. Autism--Juvenile literature. 2. Autism spectrum disorders--Juvenile literature. I. Title.
  RC553.A88A823 2012
  616.85'882--dc23
                            2011033147

TABLE OF CONTENTS

EXPERT ADVICE

Living with an autism spectrum disorder (ASD) means different things for different people. I have a doctorate in clinical psychology from the State University of New York at Buffalo, and I have worked with people with ASDs for nearly 40 years. I founded the Douglass Developmental Disabilities Center in 1972 at Douglass College of Rutgers, the State University of New Jersey. Over the years, we have served hundreds of people on the autism spectrum and their families.

Many teens with an ASD are very intelligent and do well in school. Others have intellectual disabilities or challenging behaviors that make school more difficult. Social interaction is always harder for teens with an ASD. This makes them especially vulnerable to bullying. They need help from their family, friends, and teachers to feel comfortable and safe.

Share your concerns with an adult you trust. If you have a sibling or friend with an ASD, talk to your parents or teachers when you are concerned. If you have an ASD, ask your parents or teachers to help you solve problems that come up at school or at home.

Be an advocate. Let people know that having an ASD is just a different way to be. Do your best to help people understand how to relate to your sibling or friend with an ASD. If you have an ASD, talk to your family and close friends about how you can help others understand the support you need.

Find activities everyone can enjoy. Get together with your family and friends to brainstorm activities that will be fun for everyone—whether they are on or off the spectrum.

If you are growing up with an ASD, it can be very hard to understand the social behavior of your neurotypical peers. When you don't understand why people do or say certain things, you can ask someone you trust to explain it to you.

If you have a sibling or friend with an ASD, you likely have great respect and empathy for people who are different. This ability to be sensitive to others will be a gift to you throughout your life.

However ASDs affect your life, know that you are not alone. There are support groups where you can meet teens just like you and learn how others cope with the problems you've encountered. Remember to ask for help when you need it, and never forget that you don't have to be just like everyone else to live a happy and productive life.

—Dr. Sandra Harris, PhD, Board of Governors Distinguished Service Professor Emerita, Rutgers University, New Brunswick, NJ

WHAT DOES *ASD* MEAN TO YOU? AN INTRODUCTION

Jamie sat in the living room listening to her mother trying, yet again, to explain to her brother why he should not correct his teachers. Jack just couldn't seem to get it through his head that teachers do not like it when students correct their spelling, math, or science explanations. He couldn't figure out why anyone would want to have a classroom full of students learn the material incorrectly. And besides, Jack's classmates loved when he corrected the teachers.

Jamie let out an exasperated sigh. As usual, Jack just didn't "get it." He never did. Jamie remembered her parents coming home when Jack was three and explaining all about autism spectrum disorders (ASDs). Since then, Jamie has often thought they should have just told her that having an ASD means you will never "get it."

THE TELLTALE SIGNS

Below are the typical symptoms of ASDs. Not everyone will exhibit all of these symptoms.

- Doesn't make eye contact or acknowledge other people
- Doesn't like hugging or touching
- Doesn't seem to be aware of other people's feelings
- Lives in his own world; doesn't seem to be aware of things around him
- Doesn't speak in a normal voice
- Can't participate in a conversation
- Doesn't understand how to use words correctly
- Rocks, spins, or flaps his hands; exhibits "strange" behavior
- Doesn't like change and has specific rituals he has to do
- Is always moving
- Is sensitive to lights and sounds

YOUR LIFE WITH AN ASD

You have probably heard a lot about autism, but you may not know that autism is part of a group of similar disorders called autism spectrum disorders. This book will cover the entire autism spectrum.

You may have picked up this book for many reasons. Perhaps, like Jack, you have been living with an ASD and are looking to make sense of your experiences. Or maybe, like Jamie, you have a brother or sister with an ASD you would like to better understand. You might be reading this book to learn about ASDs because your friend has one. Or perhaps you are simply curious. Recent international research suggests rates of ASDs are almost as high as 3 percent, or 1 in 33.[1] That is

LIKE NOVELS?

Check out these titles with characters who have an ASD:
Rules by Cynthia Lord

This book, a Newbery Award winner, is about Catherine and her autistic brother. Catherine knows what it means to live with a family member who needs extra attention. She's funny and endearing, and you will completely relate to her.

The Curious Incident of the Dog in the Night Time by Mark Haddon

Christopher Boone comes across a murdered dog and is blamed for it. Since Christopher has an ASD, he doesn't understand the appropriate social responses. He decides to find out who killed the dog and finds ways to navigate the complicated social world in which he lives.

approximately a 40-fold increase since 1980, when autism first appeared in the *Diagnostic and Statistical Manual of Mental Disorders* (a respected guide to diagnoses recognized by professionals in the field). At that time, the rates were only approximately 7 per 10,000.[2] It is no wonder that so many people are interested in learning about autism spectrum disorders!

ASK YOURSELF THIS

- *Where did you first hear of ASDs?*

- *What would you like to know about ASDs? What questions stick out in your mind?*

- *What do you notice about how people respond to individuals on the spectrum?*

- *If you are an individual on the spectrum, what would you like other people to know about you?*

- *If you have an ASD, what would you like to know about yourself?*

A SPECTRUM OF SYMPTOMS: DEFINING ASDs

Fourteen-year-old Jack could not understand what all the fuss was about. His big sister, Jamie, was furious with him, and he had been ordered to leave the store. Jamie had been looking for summer shorts, so they had stopped at Abercrombie and Fitch.

*Individuals who have an ASD can be confused by
social norms and expectations.*

The place was wall-to-wall with teenagers.
Even though he hated the crowd, Jack bravely
entered the sea of people and kept himself
together. Jack's mom even complimented him
on what a good job he was doing tolerating the
commotion. However, Jamie couldn't find the
shorts she wanted. With so many shoppers
digging through the clothes, the sizes were all
out of order. Jamie finally gave up and decided
to try Hollister instead. Jamie and her mom left
the store, but Jack had other ideas. He thought
maybe he could help.

Jack slipped away from his family and
began to straighten up Abercrombie and Fitch.
He grabbed an armful of clothes, laid the clothes
out on the floor, put them in size order, and then
put them back on the rack. He was happy to
be helping his sister and proud to be improving
the store. He even started fixing what the
salespeople had done wrong. Some racks held
both shirts and shorts, with jackets displayed
nearby. Jack knew that made no sense. He
started to put all of the shirts together and all of
the pants together, separate from the jackets or
other items.

When the security guard approached and
told Jack to stop what he was doing, Jack was
stunned. Jack explained that he had been

helping to organize the store. Why would anybody want him to stop that? The security guard instructed Jack to leave the store. Jack was confused and outraged. He turned to the crowd that had gathered to watch and shouted, "What is the matter with this guy?" Just then, Jack's family showed up. Jack's mom pulled the guard aside and spoke quietly to him while Jamie dragged Jack out of the store. Jamie glared at Jack and swore she would never go to the mall with him again. How ungrateful, Jack thought. How could anyone think he had done anything wrong? Why didn't the people around him ever seem to make any sense?

UNDERSTANDING ASDs

Stories like Jack's are all too familiar to individuals on the autism spectrum. To Jack,

ASDs BY THE NUMBERS

- Autism is 4 or 5 times more likely to affect boys than girls.[1]
- On average, one in 110 kids in the United States are affected by ASDs.[2]
- ASDs occur in all racial, ethnic, and socioeconomic groups.
- Prevalence of autism in the United States has increased 57 percent since 2002.[3] No one knows if this is because we have gotten better at diagnosing the disorder or if it is a true increase of the disorder itself.
- Approximately 10 percent of people with an ASD have another disorder too, such as Down syndrome, fragile X syndrome, or tuberous sclerosis.[4]

social rules and conventions were nonsensical and maddening because he just didn't see the world the way other people did. When Jack saw shirts and shorts displayed together, he saw disorder where other customers saw outfits. When Jack was reorganizing the store, he thought he was being helpful while others thought he was acting strangely. Jack also didn't understand that slipping away from his family caused them to worry about where he was and what had happened. The biggest challenge that unites all ASDs is difficulty understanding other people.

TYPES OF ASDs

Three different disorders are typically considered autism spectrum disorders: autistic disorder (autism), Asperger's syndrome, and pervasive developmental disorder not otherwise specified (PDD-NOS).

Autistic Disorder (Autism). People with autism have three types of symptoms. These types of symptoms are shared across all ASDs, though people who have an ASD other than autism experience specific variations of these core symptoms. First, like all people with an ASD, people with autism have trouble understanding other people. This can show up in many ways. People with autism may not respond to others, acting as if they are in

Social situations can be daunting for individuals with an ASD because they have difficulty understanding or relating to other people.

their own world. Some parents suspect their child with autism is deaf because the child is so unresponsive. In some cases, people with autism might treat other people as objects, even using other people's hands as tools to reach what they would like.

For other people with autism, the social deficit is subtler. Like Jack, these individuals struggle to understand that people might have a perspective different from their own. For example, a person with an ASD might really love animals and have a hard time understanding how other people could want to hunt or eat animals. This social disconnection is the hallmark feature of autism and other ASDs. In fact, Dr. Leo Kanner, the first doctor to describe patients with autism in 1947, chose the name autism because it essentially means "alone."[5]

In addition to this "aloneness," Dr. Kanner's patients had either never learned to talk or did not use their language to communicate with others. They might recite lines from nursery rhymes or make simple requests, but they did not have true conversations. This absence of or delay in communication is the second main symptom of autism. You may have seen individuals with autism use picture cards, small computers, or other devices to communicate. Other individuals with autism have large vocabularies but may have trouble with more abstract qualities of language, such as figurative language, body language, or intonation.

The third and final group of symptoms found among individuals with autism is repetitive or unusual behavior patterns. Repetitive behavior patterns can include physical behaviors such as flapping and rocking. These behaviors often occur in young children or in people who are severely impaired. Behavior patterns in higher-functioning people with an ASD include what the official diagnostic manual describes as a "restricted range of interests."[6] For example, while neurotypical people may have a passion for one subject, they tend to have a broad range of interests. However, a person with an ASD might become obsessed with one subject, such as trains or the Civil War, and not be interested in much else. Because a neurotypical person has a wider range of interests, he or she might know less about each of those interests than someone who studies only a few things. That might be why some people who are famous for knowing a lot about specific subject areas, such as Albert Einstein, Isaac Newton, or Andy Warhol, were later suspected of having some form of autism.

A symptom of ASDs that is not officially part of the diagnosis is unusual responses to sensations. People with autism often perceive sounds to be louder, visual stimuli to have more contrast, and textures to be more pronounced than people who do not have autism. Because sensations feel different to people on the autism

DID ISAAC NEWTON HAVE AN ASD?

Sir Isaac Newton is famous for his laws of motion and universal gravitation, which changed the world's understanding of physics. He may also deserve fame as one of the most accomplished individuals with an ASD. Autism expert Simon Baron-Cohen and mathematician Ioan James believe Newton displayed classic symptoms of an ASD, including a lack of connection to other people. Historical analysis reveals that Newton had few friends, hardly spoke, and was even reported to give lectures to an empty room when nobody showed up. However, his specialized interests in physics and mathematics made him one of the greatest thinkers in history.

People with ASDs perceive sensations, such as loud noises, differently than those who don't have the disorder.

spectrum, you might see these individuals respond to sensation in a way that you would not expect. For example, the tag inside a shirt might make a person with an ASD extremely uncomfortable, or the hum of an air conditioner might make it hard to pay attention in school.

The symptoms of autism tend to cause behavioral challenges. Difficulty understanding other people often results in behaviors others consider inappropriate. A classic example of a behavior problem like this is bypassing all of the empty seats on a bus to sit right next to the only other passenger. An individual with autism might not understand that the other passenger would likely feel uncomfortable or threatened by a stranger invading his or her space.

Communication difficulties can also result in problematic behaviors. Imagine individuals who can't communicate their need for food or water, or even express basic emotions. They are likely to use an inappropriate approach to get their needs met, such as screaming or kicking, if a more appropriate approach is not available. Repetitive behaviors seen in ASDs can also be associated with behavior problems. For unknown reasons, the behaviors repeated by individuals with autism sometimes include self-injurious behaviors, such as head banging or hand biting. People with an ASD sometimes use these behaviors to avoid responsibility or get attention.

Asperger's Syndrome. Just one year after Dr. Kanner published his groundbreaking study of children with autism in the United States, Dr. Hans Asperger published a similar study in Austria. While Dr. Asperger's patients shared a similar "aloneness" to Dr. Kanner's patients, their symptoms were not an exact match to Dr. Kanner's. Like the children Dr. Kanner described as autistic, Dr. Asperger's patients stood out to him because of their social challenges. In particular, he focused on their difficulty forming friendships, intense focus on special interests,

> *"It seems that for success in science or art, a dash of autism is essential."[8]*
> —Hans Asperger

and one-sided conversations. While many of Dr. Kanner's patients had cognitive delays and speech difficulties, Dr. Asperger's patients did not. In fact, Dr. Asperger's patients were so bright, talkative, and knowledgeable about their subjects of interest that he referred to them as "little professors."[7] People with Asperger's syndrome might have exceptional vocabularies and use speech productively. However, the social aspects of language (such as the give and take of a conversation) are typically still challenging for these individuals.

Pervasive Developmental Disorder Not Otherwise Specified (PDD-NOS). Some individuals suffer from the social challenges that define the autism spectrum but do not fit the definitions for either autistic disorder or Asperger's syndrome. For example, a boy might have trouble viewing things from other people's perspectives and have a speech delay, but no restricted range of interests. Or a girl might struggle with social interaction and have few interests, but have appropriate speech development. These behaviors must be substantial and distinct from shyness or a speech delay. People who show serious impairment in one or two of the three major categories that define autistic disorder or Asperger's syndrome may be diagnosed with PDD-NOS.

DIAGNOSIS

ASDs can be diagnosed in many different ways. While there is no objective medical test, trained professionals can look at an individual's development and behavior to determine whether that person has an ASD. Checklists, tests, and interviews are available to help professionals decide. Ultimately, professionals try to measure differences that family or friends of an individual notice to see if these differences are significant enough to warrant a diagnosis of an ASD. They compare the individual's symptoms to a list of official

DID YOU KNOW?

Researchers have mounting evidence that ASDs can be identified in toddlers by following their eye gaze. Toddlers who later develop an ASD prefer to look at mouths or any place where motion and sound occur together. Toddlers who later are found to be typically developing prefer to look at eyes.

criteria to determine whether an ASD is the cause.

A psychologist, psychiatrist, pediatrician, pediatric neurologist, developmental pediatrician, or a professional from a related field might be trained to administer an assessment. If you suspect you or someone you know has an ASD, ask a parent or a counselor at your school to help get you to the right professional. While you might be concerned about being labeled, or about how people will see you if you are diagnosed with an ASD, you can choose not to tell people you don't think will understand. Getting the diagnosis is important because it will allow you to get treatment that will help you.

ASK YOURSELF THIS

- *Do you think you or someone you know may have an ASD? Why?*

- *What would you do if you suspected someone had an ASD?*

- *If you were the security guard in the store, how would you have reacted to Jack?*

- *If you were Jamie, would you go back to the mall with Jack?*

- *If you were Jack, what would you say to Jamie?*

WHY ME? CAUSES AND PREVENTION

For once, Jamie couldn't wait to do her homework assignment for health class. She had firsthand experience, so it would be an easy A. Ms. Felhall had no idea the topic Jamie chose was one close to her heart: autism spectrum disorders.

The cause of ASDs is unknown, though researchers continue to seek answers. Many factors may contribute to an individual developing a disorder.

Now, sitting at her desk at home, Jamie did an Internet search for ASD. She needed sources, and then she could add her own thoughts on the matter. She typed in "ASD" and millions of hits came up. OK, maybe this would be harder than she thought. Where would she even begin? Jamie realized that even though she had lived with autism since Jack was born, she had never really asked questions about it. Maybe now was a good time to start. She could start with her parents.

Jumping down the stairs two at a time, she yelled, "Mom!" Her mom turned the corner in the hallway and said, "Shhhh," pointing at Jack in the living room. Jack sat cross-legged on the floor, practicing the relaxation exercises his counselor had given him. Quieter, Jamie said, "Mom, I have a report due about autism. Can I ask you some questions?"

Her mom stepped back in surprise. "Of course you can. Go ahead and shoot." They walked into the kitchen, and as Jamie slipped onto the stool by the breakfast bar, she realized she didn't even know where to start.

Then it hit her. She should start at the beginning.

"What caused Jack's autism?" After she asked the question, Jamie wondered why she had never asked before. She went on, "Could it have been prevented?" Jamie felt a little guilty about asking these questions. They hadn't come out the way she'd meant them—it sort of sounded like Jamie was blaming her parents. But she knew her questions were important, and she knew Jack's autism was not her parents' fault.

Her mom took a deep breath. "Well, like everything about ASDs, it's complicated."

WHY?

If you or someone you know has been diagnosed with an ASD, the first question you might ask is "Why did this happen?" Researchers are not completely sure what leads to the development of an ASD, but they do know that ASDs may be caused by a combination of genetic and environmental factors.

GENES

You have probably learned a little bit about genes in biology class. Genes are made up of proteins that work like computer programs to tell your body how to develop. However, genes do not shape your development by themselves. They prepare you to have a range of possible features, but your environment determines what exactly will occur.

GENETICS

Recent scientific studies have shown that some people are genetically predisposed to develop autism.

Scientific studies of twins show that ASDs are linked to genetics.

The best evidence for the influence of genetics on autism is twin studies. When doing twin studies, researchers compare identical twins with fraternal twins. Identical twins share exactly the same genes, so any genetically inherited disorder will show up in both twins. In contrast, fraternal twins do not share more genes than other siblings. Twin studies show that approximately 90 percent of ASD cases are determined by genetics.[1] That leaves 10 percent of cases to be explained by the environment or by genes that are not yet identified. Researchers do not know exactly what it is about the environment that makes the difference.

ENVIRONMENTAL FACTORS

Researchers do not yet know what environmental factors determine whether a person will develop an ASD. Some experts believe babies exposed to chemicals in the womb are more likely to develop an ASD. For example, mothers who, in the 1950s and 1960s, took the sedative thalidomide while pregnant were more likely to have a child who developed an ASD.[2] Other experts have showed that being exposed to pollutants such as mercury or metals could act as an environmental trigger for ASDs.

ONE CAUSE OF MULTIPLE DISORDERS

One of the complications in identifying the causes of ASDs is that we cannot yet separate different disorders from one another. There is no blood test or other biological marker we can use to conclude that one child has one particular ASD and a different child has another. That means children who have different causes for their symptoms end up being lumped together in research studies because their symptoms resemble one another. Researchers are working very hard to separate out individuals with varied types of autism spectrum disorders for research and treatment purposes, but that is not yet possible.

WHAT DOES NOT CAUSE ASDs?

There has been a seemingly endless stream of theories about what causes autism. Two false theories in particular have caused significant societal problems.

In 1967, Bruno Bettelheim published a book called *The Empty Fortress*. In this book, Bettelheim argues that autism is caused by cold, non-affectionate mothers. He referred to these women as "refrigerator mothers," a term coined by Dr. Kanner.[3] This book resulted in a great deal of self-blame and finger-pointing at the mothers of autistic children. Treatment was misdirected toward teaching parents how to be warmer with their children. However, there was never any scientific support for this theory. In the end, both parents and professionals wholeheartedly dismissed these ideas.

Similarly, Dr. Andrew Wakefield published a study in 1998 suggesting that the measles-mumps-rubella vaccine played a role in causing

WHEN IS AN ASD NOT AN ASD?

For approximately 15 percent of people experiencing ASD symptoms, other neurological disorders are causing those symptoms.[4] Some of these disorders include genetic problems such as fragile X syndrome, neurological problems such as tuberous sclerosis, or metabolic problems such as untreated phenylketonuria.

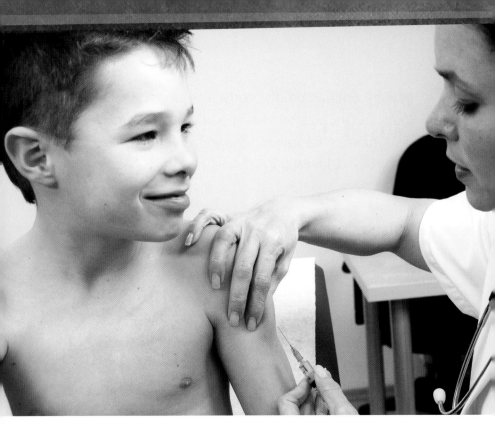

The measles-mumps-rubella vaccine does not cause ASDs. It is important to keep up with vaccinations.

ASDs. This prompted many parents to refuse to vaccinate their children. Unfortunately, many children who did not receive recommended vaccines contracted preventable diseases such as whooping cough and measles.

After Dr. Wakefield published his findings, his colleagues at universities around the world tried to find out if they would get the same result if they studied the same question. Study after study found no relationship between vaccines and ASDs. In 2010, Dr. Wakefield was accused of violating ethical and scientific guidelines in how he conducted his study. The British General Medical Council found him guilty of academic dishonesty. The *Lancet*, the journal that had originally published Wakefield's study, finally retracted the article.

ASK YOURSELF THIS

- *What theories about the causes of ASDs make the most sense to you? Do you have a theory of your own? If so, what is it?*

- *What environmental factors do you think might cause ASDs?*

- *If the cause of ASDs were identified and it became preventable, do you think we should prevent them?*

- *Dr. Wakefield published a study that had a widespread impact and turned out to be based on unsound research practices. Does this make you question other findings? Why or why not?*

- *When you read articles about ASDs, how do you decide whether the information is reliable?*

4

FIX IT! CURRENT TREATMENTS FOR ASDs

Jamie stood in front of the class. Speaking in public always made her so nervous she could barely breathe. Ms. Felhall looked at her kindly from behind her desk.

"Start whenever you're ready, Jamie," she said with a gentle smile.

If you have an ASD or know someone who does, informing others about symptoms and treatments can help raise awareness.

Jamie smiled back at her teacher and felt a little better. She reminded herself that her report was good enough that Ms. Felhall had asked her to talk about it in front of the class. With a deep breath, Jamie read her report aloud.

When she was through, the class was quiet.

"Are there any questions?" Ms. Felhall asked.

No one answered. Jamie swallowed nervously—had she read too fast? Or maybe it was just a dumb report. Jamie looked down at her feet. She wouldn't mind if the floor just swallowed her up.

Ms. Felhall cleared her throat and Jamie looked up. At least five hands were raised. Jamie felt exhilarated. Maybe it wasn't such a dumb report after all.

She pointed to Justin, a boy who sat behind her. "Yes?"

"So, is there anything you can do for ASDs?"

Jamie exhaled. She realized that her report had not covered treatment options, so she was glad Justin had asked.

"These days, my brother just sees a psychologist and an occupational therapist. Also, a behavior therapist works with my parents and his teachers. When my brother was younger, he had special teachers who came to the house every afternoon to work with him. He also had a speech therapist, a ton of medications, and was on a special diet."

Justin's eyebrows went up. "That's a lot of stuff."

Jamie nodded. "Yeah, but I think all of it helped. And if it helps, it is definitely worth it!"

A TREATMENT THAT WORKS

Because no one knows the exact cause of ASDs or how to prevent them, this makes them difficult to treat. An effective treatment for any ASD would have to help in many areas, including social skills, language skills, and behavior problems. There have been at least as many proposed treatments for people with ASDs as proposed causes. Treatment ideas range from exposing individuals with ASDs to different kinds of animals, to placing them in rooms with a lot of oxygen, to highly invasive medical procedures designed to remove toxins from the blood. Unfortunately, few of these treatments have solid research supporting them. However, one ASD treatment does have evidence to show its effectiveness: applied behavior analysis (ABA).

APPLIED BEHAVIOR ANALYSIS

Applied behavior analysis is the science of learning and human behavior. It uses what we know about how people learn to help reduce the symptoms of ASDs. One thing that helps people learn is breaking down skills into small parts. For example, people do not learn to play tennis by walking onto the court in the middle of a set. Tennis instruction usually begins with the very basic skill of how to properly grasp a tennis racket. Once the student masters this skill, the instructor moves on to teach another basic skill. Teaching progresses step-by-step, which is an essential part of ABA as well.

Another important part of ABA is providing rewards for the behaviors you would like to teach. Students are praised for performing at their current best level, whatever that may be. Behavior analysts carefully plan when rewards will be delivered based on

THE ABCs OF ABA

Here are a few ABA terms you may come across:

Reinforcement. This is a reward for good behavior. A reinforcement is something that happens as a result of a behavior that will make that behavior more likely to occur again.

Extinction. This is when we stop reinforcing an unwanted behavior, such as throwing a tantrum, so that behavior gradually stops.

Prompt. A prompt is a little extra help with an instruction to make sure the student gets the right answer.

ABA helps individuals with ASDs develop social skills, such as interacting with classmates at school.

the current needs and progress of each individual with an ASD.

ABA is a science. Every behavior change can be measured. For example, we might count how many times a person with an ASD asks for an item using words instead of grabbing, or how many times a student with an ASD talks to classmates in the cafeteria. Measuring these behaviors allows the behaviorist to track change in a fair and unbiased manner, leading to accurate decisions about whether a treatment plan is working.

It is impossible to give a single description of ABA because it has so many forms. For example, discrete trial instruction (DTI) is a type of ABA that involves a lot of repetition and may look a bit mechanical. For example, students may be asked to "touch red," or put their hands on the red item in an array, ten times in succession. This allows practice and ensures the students can correctly follow the direction given. In contrast, pivotal response training (PRT) is a type of ABA that follows a student's lead and interest, capturing spontaneous opportunities to teach skills and concepts. For example, a PRT student learning about the color red might ask for an item and be told the teacher has placed it in the "red" box. This box would be placed next to containers of other colors. To get the item he or she wants, the student has to correctly identify the color red. To build practice opportunities, many items the student likes might be hidden in red containers.

DTI and PRT are just two of many strategies that might be used within an ABA educational program. These two strategies provide examples from each extreme of the teacher-directed versus student-directed ABA instructional spectrum. ABA might be used one-on-one, or it might be used in a group. It might be done face-to-face with lots of vocal and gestural interaction between therapist and student, or it might be done with the therapist sitting or standing close behind the student, using only hand gestures to cue certain behaviors. When watching ABA, you will notice the breakdown of skills into small parts and rewards provided when desired skills are achieved. Furthermore, progress in ABA educational programs is carefully measured and analyzed.

ABA is based on the work of B. F. Skinner. Skinner extensively studied behavior change

HOW CAN I USE ABA?

You can use ABA principles to help yourself or someone you care about with an ASD. Here are some ideas:

Reinforcement: When someone you care about who has an ASD does something you'd like to see more of, do something you know they would like. You can even use reinforcement with yourself. For example, if you really like music, reward yourself with a song each time you meet a goal.

Extinction: If a person you know with an ASD behaves in a way you don't like, do not provide the outcome you think he or she is trying to achieve. For example, if your brother screams to get your attention, ignore him until he asks politely.

Prompt: If someone with an ASD needs to practice a new skill, give him or her a little help. For example, if your classmate with an ASD has trouble finding a seat in the cafeteria, tell him you will save him a seat and stand up so he can easily see the seat. If you have trouble remembering which classrooms to go to in which order, write the classroom numbers down. The list can serve as a prompt for where to go next.

The methods of ABA are based on the work of B. F. Skinner, one of the world's most influential psychologists, shown here in 1971.

and learning in controlled laboratory settings. In 1959, Teodoro Ayllon and Jack Michael applied the principles of behavior that Skinner had demonstrated in a laboratory to real-life problems experienced by patients in the psychiatric ward of a hospital. Skinner's strategies proved effective in creating behavior change in the real world. This marked the beginning of the field of applied behavior analysis. Clinical researchers continued to apply Skinner's behavioral principles and repeatedly found them to be effective.

Years later, in 1987, psychologist Ivar Lovaas adapted ABA to the treatment of children with autism spectrum disorders. He used IQ tests and behavioral measures to show that, by the beginning of first grade, about half of the children who received ABA were able to go to a regular education classroom and not seem very different from their classmates. In comparison, none of the students who did not receive the treatment (we call that a comparison or control group) were able to do so. When Lovaas and his colleagues tried these strategies with other groups of children with autism, they got similar results.

Parents or teachers can implement ABA programs, and you can even learn to use these strategies to change your own behavior. A Board Certified Behavior Analyst (BCBA) should always oversee an ABA program. To find a

SKINNER ON REWARDS

In *Schedules of Reinforcement*, B. F. Skinner tells how rewards affect behavior:

When an organism acts upon the environment in which it lives, it changes that environment in ways which often affect the organism itself. Some of these changes are what the layman calls rewards, or what are now generally referred to technically as reinforcers: when [rewards] follow behavior in this way, they increase the likelihood that the organism will behave in the same way again.[1]

BCBA, go to the Behavior Analyst Certification Board Web site.

ASK YOURSELF THIS

- *Have you ever tried to change someone's behavior? What strategies did you use?*

- *Do you think it is important to use only treatments that have been well researched? Why or why not?*

- *Do you believe you can measure behavior clearly enough to research behavior change? Why or why not?*

- *If you have an ASD, what forms of ABA do you think would work best for you and why? If your sibling or friend has an ASD, what forms of ABA would you like him or her to try and why?*

- *Has anyone ever tried to get you to change your behavior? What worked and what didn't?*

5

WHAT ELSE MIGHT WORK? ALTERNATIVE TREATMENTS

Jamie bumped into her dad as she bounded up the stairs.

"Whoa, where's the fire?" he said to her back. Jamie smiled and rolled her eyes. Her dad was so cheesy sometimes.

Jamie stopped at the top of the stairs and called back down, "I need to check a recipe on my computer. I want to make sure that Jack can have it on his special diet."

He laughed. "Well don't hurt yourself." Her dad turned to walk down the rest of the stairs, then whirled around. "Wait, recipe?"

Jamie nodded. "Yep! I'm making dinner tonight!"

Her dad grabbed his chest and staggered back, pretending to have a hard time breathing. "You're making dinner without being asked?" he gasped.

Jamie couldn't help but giggle. "Daa-ad." She rolled her eyes again. "I'm celebrating. I got an A on my report, and some of my classmates even asked me questions after class. I told them about Jack's gluten-free, casein-free diet, and they got curious and I got hungry." She shrugged nonchalantly. "So I decided to make dinner." Jamie flipped around and ran into her room. She jotted down the recipe on a fluorescent pink sticky note.

Her mom was at the stove stirring the pasta sauce Jamie had made. "Hands off!" said Jamie, and her mom backed away with her hands up. Jamie saw the smile between her mom and her dad. Jamie remembered when it had been so hard to find foods Jack could eat. Now, there were entire gluten-free sections in the grocery store.

Her dad said, "So, what's on the menu tonight?"

Jamie answered, "Rice pasta with my special tomato sauce, sautéed Swiss chard, and for dessert, applesauce." She beamed.

Her parents smiled back. Her mom said, "That sounds like a perfect meal from a perfect sister."

POPULAR ALTERNATIVE TREATMENTS

ABA is the only treatment for autism spectrum disorders that is documented to work. However, a variety of other treatments are widely used. Some of the treatments described below have some research supporting them, though their effectiveness is debated.

BE CAREFUL OF CHELATION

One proposed treatment for ASDs, called chelation, involves an effort to remove toxins from the blood. Chemicals designed to remove lead, mercury, and other toxic metals from the blood are administered to the patient intravenously. These chemicals have not been tested for use in individuals with ASDs. Professionals who work with individuals with ASDs do not endorse this treatment. At least one boy has died as a result of chelation.[1]

TEACCH

Treatment and Education of Autistic and Communication Related Handicapped Children (TEACCH) is an approach to the treatment of individuals with autism based on a perceived "culture of autism." According to TEACCH professionals, individuals with ASDs thrive when their environment provides structure, organization, and predictability. To this end, TEACCH practitioners organize spaces in a way that makes it easier for the person in that space to work. For example, if a task should be completed in a specific order, the task materials are set out in that order. The TEACCH model also relies on visual cues—such as pictures, written cues, and gestures—to aid in communication. TEACCH professionals believe people with ASDs often have a strong preference for visual information. Schedules are another example of a visual aid used with this approach. TEACCH has some limited research supporting its effectiveness but needs more research conducted with carefully planned studies.

RELATIONSHIP-BASED APPROACHES

Some treatments for ASDs are based on building interpersonal relationships. While professionals are committed to exploring relationship-based approaches, these approaches do not have significant research support at this time. Nevertheless, they are popular among families of individuals with an ASD and are fairly widely used.

Relationship development intervention (RDI) focuses on building social skills and encouraging social interaction. It particularly emphasizes relying on nonverbal cues within those interactions. For example, part of an RDI approach for an early learner might target gaze following. A parent might hide an object in one of two containers and use only his or her gaze to direct the student to the correct container. Parents are trained to do structured RDI activities with their children.

DIR/Floortime is a well-publicized intervention for ASDs that also emphasizes social interaction. DIR stands for "developmental, individual difference, relationship-based," which highlights the main tenets of this approach. In contrast to the RDI approach, DIR/Floortime aims to make a general change in the child's social connectedness, rather than focusing on specific sets of skills. This approach is also less structured than RDI, allowing the student to choose the activity. DIR/ Floortime practitioners often place themselves between students and their desired item or activity, forcing students to interact with them.

RDI encourages social interaction.

For example, a DIR/Floortime practitioner might block the doorway to a room a student with an ASD wants to enter. The teacher might demand a "toll" in the form of a high five in order to enter the room. This requires the student to exit his or her own world briefly and connect with another person in order to move forward with a desired activity. The effectiveness of this approach is difficult to measure. As a result, there is little research to support the use of DIR/Floortime.

SPECIFIC THERAPIES

Speech therapy, occupational therapy, and physical therapy have long been used to support the development of individuals with autism spectrum disorders. Some therapists work with behavior analysts or other professionals to provide treatment within an ABA framework. For example, a speech therapist might use a verbal behavior (VB) approach (a strand of ABA focused on how language is used) to teach students to make requests or answer questions.

An occupational therapist might use an approach that supports the development of fine motor skills. Because each type of occupational therapy has so many different approaches, it is impossible to gather a strong body of research for the field as a whole.

SAY WHAT YOU MEAN

Verbal behavior (VB) programs focus specifically on helping people with ASDs develop the language skills they generally lack. VB experts demonstrate that just because a person knows a word does not mean that person can use the word to communicate his or her thoughts or needs. Teachers in VB programs want to show their students that appropriate use of language will get them what they want. Students in VB programs spend a lot of time learning how to request things and answer questions.

MEDICATION

While there is no pill to cure ASDs,

certain medications may help with some symptoms. Medications that ease anxiety or control obsessive behaviors have been used to treat people with ASDs. Antidepressants and antipsychotic medications have also been used to help with behavior and mood challenges and to cut down on repetitive and obsessive behaviors. And finally, some stimulants used to treat attention deficit disorder have helped to ease symptoms of ASDs. All of these medications have side effects, so be sure to thoroughly discuss the benefits and risks with your doctor.

ALTERNATIVE THERAPIES: WHAT YOU DON'T KNOW MIGHT HURT YOU!

Many popular and widely used treatments for autism suffer from limited research supporting their use. The gluten-free, casein-free diet, dietary supplements, and auditory integration training are all widely used interventions based on limited research. While these treatments are unlikely to harm an individual on the autism spectrum, some proposed treatments for autism can be dangerous. Before trying any alternative treatment, gather as much information as you can from an unbiased source, such as the Association for Science in Autism Treatment.

Auditory integration training (AIT) aims to help individuals with hypersensitive hearing. Like other alternative therapies, there is little evidence to support its effectiveness.

This organization has a very thorough Web site that reviews proposed treatments for ASDs and warns of potential risks.

PROGNOSIS

While prognosis varies from person to person, research has taught us three lessons about the prognosis for individuals with ASDs:

1. The earlier intervention can be started, the better the prognosis.
2. Early intensive behavioral intervention usually leads to the best outcome.
3. Using ABA-based approaches boosts your chances of having a positive outcome.

Some individuals with an ASD grow up to be highly productive members of society who have their own families and function with minimal assistance. Unfortunately, some individuals with an ASD never achieve independence and will always require support from other people. Most individuals with an ASD fall somewhere between those two outcomes. It is especially distressing that once young people on the spectrum graduate from high school,

AUDITORY INTEGRATION TRAINING

Auditory integration training (AIT) is a treatment that many believe helps people with hypersensitive hearing. This is a common symptom of ASDs. AIT involves having a person with an ASD listen to specially chosen music that often changes volume and frequency. There is little evidence that AIT is effective, but the treatment is widely used.

the resources for learning new skills are poorly funded and often difficult to access.

ASK YOURSELF THIS

- *If you or someone you know has an ASD, what types of treatments have you/he/she tried? Which do you think were the most effective?*

- *Are you or anyone else you know with an ASD on medications? How do they help or not help?*

- *What do you think schools should offer for ASD help?*

IS TREATMENT NECESSARY?

There is an "anti-cure" movement among individuals with autism who argue that they do not have a disease, but rather an alternative way of life. Consider the following quote by Frank Klein, a high-functioning person with autism:

Autism itself is not the enemy . . . the barriers to development that are included with autism are the enemy. The retardation that springs from a lack of development is the enemy. The sensory problems that are often themselves the barriers are the enemy. These things are not part of who the child is . . . they are barriers to who the child is meant to be, according to the developmental blueprint. Work with the child's strengths to overcome the weaknesses, and work within the autism, not against it, to overcome the developmental barriers. You do not have to wipe all of us out ("cure autism") to solve the problems that the low-functioning autistics face.[2]

- *How responsive is your doctor or team of doctors when you have questions about ASDs?*

- *What alternative treatments for ASDs are you interested in trying? Why?*

WHO GETS IT: PUBLIC UNDERSTANDING AND SUPPORT

Jack worked diligently on the project he and his classmates were supposed to complete that afternoon. While he focused on his assignment, Jack thought he must be the only one doing any work! Jack could hear his classmates whispering to one another about plans for the weekend, discussing where they would go and who would be invited. Jack could not understand why they didn't just do their work during work time and socialize at lunch or after school. At the same time, he wished someone would include him.

Jack was abruptly jarred from his thoughts when, suddenly, the fire alarm sounded. He panicked. The sound was unbearable. It felt like a million bees were stinging his ears at once. Jack's heart raced. His head pounded. He thought he might pass out, but he couldn't move even to put his head down. Two of Jack's classmates who had known Jack since elementary school raced over to him. Each grabbed one of his arms and escorted him outside to safety. They had learned about Jack's disorder each year in school and always looked out for Jack's needs and safety. Years of experience with fire drills had taught them that the sound of the alarm meant Jack needed help.

CURRENT SUPPORT

In the early years after Dr. Kanner had first identified autism as a distinct disorder, very few individuals with that diagnosis lived at home with their families. Instead, individuals with developmental challenges including autism were typically sent to live in institutional settings. This meant that people rarely met someone with a developmental disability, much less a person with an ASD. In the 1970s when people with many kinds of developmental disorders were moved from large institutions to community-based settings, people on the autism spectrum were included in that change. Federal legislators wrote laws to ensure that children on the autism spectrum were included in public schools and in programs designed specifically for people with ASDs. While individuals with ASDs still face significant challenges, they now have a variety of supportive resources available to them as a result of this broader inclusion in the community.

CHALLENGES FOR PEOPLE WITH ASDs

Even if teens with an ASD get the support they need through high school and college, they face a lack of resources devoted to career development and independent living after graduation. There are not enough group homes and supervised apartments to allow all individuals with an ASD the opportunity to live independently. It is also difficult for many people with an ASD to have a meaningful career or even find a job. Teens living with an ASD need their neurotypical peers to advocate for them

With the help of a job coach, many adults with an ASD are able to work and be productive.

and help them find ways to live, work, and contribute to society as adults.

JOB OPPORTUNITIES FOR ADULTS

Historically, someone with an ASD would have had little hope of earning money independently as an adult. Today, individuals with ASDs have a range of options. Some individuals on the spectrum obtain and maintain their own jobs. Others need assistance called "supported employment" to work successfully. Job coaches assist these individuals in the workplace to help them work as independently as possible. For example, a job coach can help break down a large task that seems overwhelming to the individual with an ASD into smaller, more manageable parts. A job coach can also anticipate challenges for the client with an ASD and help develop coping strategies for those situations. Due to increased inclusion and awareness, a variety of supportive resources are in place to help individuals with ASDs find employment.

COLLEGE ACCOMMODATIONS

Today, society understands that individuals with special needs often have wonderful gifts and skills to contribute to society. Colleges are more likely to admit individuals with ASDs, knowing that even if they have a hard time with some aspects of the curriculum, they will be able to benefit from and contribute to other

EMPLOYMENT STATISTICS

According to the National Longitudinal Transition Study 2, a ten-year study of youth who received special education services, young adults with ASDs are less likely to work than members of most other disability groups. The study was completed in 2009 when participants were ages 23–26:

32.5 percent of young adults with [ASDs . . .] worked for pay versus an average of 59.0 percent for all respondents. Only one disability group had a lower rate of employment participation.

[. . .]

29.0 percent of young adults with [ASDs] were looking for work if they were unemployed compared to 47.7 percent for all participants.[1]

areas of the curriculum. To ensure the success of ASD students, colleges around the country are offering programs specifically for them. These programs offer mentoring professors, supplemental coursework designed to focus on organizational skills, and support groups.

LIVING ARRANGEMENTS

Thankfully, the days when individuals on the autism spectrum were "shipped off" to some type of institution are gone. Today, adults on the autism spectrum have a few options. They might live independently just like any other adult. If this is not possible, an individual on the spectrum might choose to live in a supervised apartment. This usually means the residents are mostly independent but a support person visits periodically to check on things. That support person might offer help organizing and paying bills, keeping the refrigerator stocked, or other things specific to the needs of the residents. Other individuals with ASDs need more support than this. They might live in a group home. This is a home with a group of residents that have 24-hour staff ensuring their safety and supporting their routine. Group homes are sometimes set up with job coaches and transportation to and from work.

LIVING INDEPENDENTLY

According to a National Autistic Society survey of more than 450 children and adults with autism in the United Kingdom, 70 percent of adults with autism are unable to live on their own. Only 3 percent of adults with autism live completely unaided.[2] Others may live with family or in residential care facilities.

HELP FROM THE COMMUNITY

Many communities now offer special accommodations for people on the spectrum. For example, because of a restricted range of interests, it can be hard for individuals on the spectrum to wait for extended periods of time. While neurotypical people are waiting in line, they might make up games, people watch, chat, or enjoy the scenery. Having fewer interests can make waiting a challenge for individuals on the spectrum. To accommodate this challenge, many theme parks now offer passes for individuals on the spectrum so they can go straight to the front of the line!

Movie theaters also offer special accommodations for individuals with ASDs. Because movie theaters typically play the movies at a high volume and use huge screens with bright visuals, this can be a challenge for individuals with autism. To improve the ASD person's theater experience, some theaters now offer "sensory friendly" movies. At a sensory friendly movie, the lights stay on to make the colors on the screen less jarring, the volume stays low so it is not overwhelming, and there are no previews. People can also bring in their own snacks, making it easier on those who follow special diets. Most important, moviegoers can get up and stroll if they need to, and no one will yell at them to sit down or stay quiet.

FAMILY SUPPORT

One benefit of the increase in the prevalence of ASDs is that it is easier to find friends who know about these disorders. It can be especially hard on siblings if they don't have friends or classmates who understand their experiences with a brother or a sister on the spectrum. To ensure that every sibling can find someone to talk to who understands, the University of Washington has created the Sibling Support Project. This program created Sibshops, or sibling supportive discussion groups. The Sibling Support Project trains professionals around the country to run these groups. If there are no discussion groups in your area, find online chat opportunities and other resources on their Web site, www.siblingsupport.org.

In addition, many recreation centers, such as Jewish Community Centers, YMCAs, YWCAs, and even health clubs, have begun offering special recreational activities just

Children with autism wear their pride on World Autism Awareness Day in New Delhi, India.

for families with special needs. For example, these clubs may have monthly craft activities or weekly swim sessions just for families with special needs.

AUTISM AWARENESS MONTH

April is autism awareness month in the United States. The goal of autism awareness month is to help community members learn about ASDs and the important issues facing people affected by an ASD and their families. Activities might include fund-raisers, guest speakers sharing information about ASDs at schools and libraries, or individuals with ASDs going to the US Congress or their state legislature to press for the passage of important bills. The number of potential autism awareness activities is infinite, but the important goals are to help the general public become knowledgeable about and comfortable with ASDs, to teach the public how to better respond to individuals on the spectrum, and to meet fund-raising and legislative goals.

It is autism awareness activities such as these that lead to a broader understanding and appreciation of people with ASDs and the unique challenges they face.

ASK YOURSELF THIS

- *What are some ASD-friendly recreation activities near you?*

- *In what ways does your community support people with ASDs?*

- *How can you reach out to people to educate them about ASDs?*

- *What sorts of things can you do to make people with ASDs feel more welcome and included?*

- *Have you come across people working in the community who might have had a special need? How have you interacted with them?*

SURVIVAL TOOLS: TEENS ON THE SPECTRUM

Jack caught another glimpse of that pretty girl, Kerry. He noticed she was sitting alone at the lunch table. "Here is my chance!" he thought. Jack walked over to her and sat down next to her. Right next to her. Kerry looked a little startled, scooted a few feet away from him, and said, "Hi, Jack." He said hi to her and thought this was his in. Kerry waved at friends as they walked by, and Jack struggled to think of something to say. While he thought about it, her friends came and sat with her. One friend squeezed between Kerry and Jack. Jack was furious. "DON'T YOU SEE I AM SITTING WITH KERRY?" Jack yelled. The whole cafeteria turned to look at him.

"Jack, you didn't even say a word to me. How was I supposed to know you were sitting here to talk to me?" Kerry said.

Jack just looked at her, confused.

FRIENDSHIPS AND DATING

The only thing harder than being a teenager is being a teenager on the spectrum! As a general rule, people are difficult to understand. If a girl goes on a date with a guy, and she really likes him, and he sends her flowers the next day, she might tell her friends it was the most romantic gesture in the world. If a girl goes on a date with a guy, and she did not enjoy herself, and he sends her flowers the next day, she might tell her friends he is a psycho stalker and plot to get rid of him. How is the guy to know whether or not to send those flowers? These are the types

A peer mentor can help you deal with social challenges at school.

of judgment calls all teenagers must make, and they are not easy.

    If you are an individual with an ASD, these judgments can be even more complicated. You might have more trouble reading the girl's reactions during the date or reading her response after she gets the flowers. It is enough to make your head spin! While there is no good solution to these challenges, the following are some tips that might help.

- Get a peer mentor. Do you have a friend with strong social skills? Do you have a sibling, cousin, or neighbor whom you trust? If so, ask this person if she or he would mind helping you figure things out. For example, you can ask this person for advice about figuring out where to sit at lunch, or whether you know a person well enough to invite him or her to do something after school, or whether to trust someone who has invited you out. If you can get someone who attends your school to help, that is even better, because that person will know the personalities involved. If you do not have a person in mind, ask a trusted teacher or school counselor for help matching you up with a mentor.

- Work on those social skills. While it is true that having an ASD means you will always have more trouble in social situations than other people, you can improve your social skills if you keep at it. Consider participating in a social skills group or working with a counselor or a behavior analyst to help you understand the interactions going on around you. Resources are available that you can use on

UNDERSTANDING HUMOR

Understanding humor can be a tremendous challenge for individuals with ASDs. Humor often relies on words with multiple meanings and nonverbal cues. These areas of comprehension are particularly hard-hit by ASDs. Educational programs specifically geared to target these skills can help individuals with ASDs improve their sense of humor.

your own, but it is best if you have other people with whom to discuss these skills. This will give you the confidence and skills to navigate confusing social situations.

MANAGING PHYSICAL CHANGES

During the teenage years, your body is constantly surprising you. It might seem like your body changed completely overnight! These changes can be tough to manage. The following are tips to help you figure out how to respond to your new physique.

- Educate yourself. You will be much more comfortable with the changes that go on in your body if you know what to expect. Talk to a parent, an older sibling, or a counselor and ask them to let you know what might happen next. There are also lots of books that review what happens in your body during this period of time. Know what is coming!

- Keep physical changes to yourself. Even though every teenager is going through the same things, nobody wants to hear about it. It is one of those silly rules people without ASDs follow that makes no sense. If you notice a change in someone else's body, that person does not want you to look at it or comment on it. If you experience a change in your body, you should try not to draw attention to it. Again, it is a silly rule, as all young people go through these changes, but it is true that everyone wants their physical changes kept to themselves.

BULLYING

Basically, bullying is being mean to someone to establish power over them. Bullying can happen online, on the playground, in school, and before and after school. In a recent study of teenagers with Asperger's syndrome, researchers found 100 percent of the kids had been bullied.[1] Given this finding, a person with an ASD will likely have to deal with bullying at some point.

Bullying involves three types of participants: bullies, victims, and bystanders. The key to disrupting the bullying is for the victims and the bystanders to speak up. Work with a trusted adult to prevent bullying by staying near supervising adults, training classmates to tell

BULLYING STATISTICS

- 15–25 percent of students in the United States say they have been bullied.
- 15–25 percent of students in the United States say they have bullied someone else.
- Kids who bully are more likely to drop out of school, smoke, and drink alcohol.
- As many as 160,000 kids will stay home from school today because they are afraid of being bullied.
- 60 percent of boys who bullied in middle school had at least one criminal conviction by the time they were 24.[2]
  Bullying hurts everyone involved. By sticking up for someone, you may be helping many people!

bullies they do not like what is happening, and having an escape and follow-up plan if you are being bullied.

If you are reading this as a friend of someone with an ASD, stick up for people when you see any teasing going on. If you feel at all in danger, make sure to go to a teacher or other adult to intervene—never put yourself in danger. However, if someone says something bad about someone or teases another person for being different and you do not feel endangered, you can take a stand because you know better what "different" means. You have enough information to stop that sort of ignorance in its tracks. You can stand up for your friend with an ASD (or anyone being teased!) and let those around you know bullying is not okay. It takes courage to do this, but one person standing up can encourage others to do the same.

DON'T GO IT ALONE

Many bullies target people who are alone. Because individuals with ASDs have trouble making friends, they are often alone and might be targeted. One strategy to protect yourself might be to ask teachers for help setting up a buddy system so you are not alone very often. This buddy system can take the form of a book club that meets during recess, a chess club, or other group activity. A structured activity allows you to be with other students even if you are not great at meeting people on your own.

ASK YOURSELF THIS

- *What social skills do you know you need to work on? How will you work on them?*

- *Have you ever been bullied because of your ASD? How did you handle the situation?*

- *If you have an ASD, how do you feel about dating? If you do not have an ASD, how do you think you would feel about romantic relationships if you did?*

- *Who would you choose as your peer mentor? Why?*

- *What would you do if someone was bullying your friend or sibling with an ASD?*

LEARNING TO COPE: SIBLINGS WITH AN ASD

Jamie called her mom again. The last few stragglers from the volleyball game were packing up, and Jamie felt a twisting in her gut. She hoped she wouldn't have to hitch a ride with the coach again.

"Pick up, pick up, pick up," Jamie chanted as the phone rang on the other end. It went to voice mail again. Jamie hung up without leaving a message. She knew exactly why her mom wasn't here. The same reason her mom could hardly come to any of her games.

Jamie fished around in her gym bag again, fiddling with her knee pads and volleyball uniform to look like she was busy doing something. She tried to hold them back but tears pricked her eyes. Why was she always the last one at the games?

Her coach walked over and said, "Hey Jamie, do you need a ride?"

Jamie swallowed and stood up. Just as she was about to answer, her mom swooped into the gym, face flushed and hair flying. Jamie sighed in relief.

"No thanks, Coach," she said looking down.

Jamie's mom reached them. "How did she do?" she asked, out of breath. "I wish I could have been here."

Coach said, "She was great, as usual. She's not afraid to dig deep!"

Jamie's mom put her hand on her shoulder. "That's our Jamie—a hard worker! We don't know what we'd do without her."

Jamie blushed. She felt both angry and proud. She shrugged and said, "See you, Coach."

Jamie and her mother walked out the door. "Sorry I'm late, honey. Jack . . ." She rolled her eyes at Jamie. Jamie understood. But she and her parents had made a deal that she would talk to them when she was frustrated.

"I know, Mom, but I'm still upset. I really wish you could have come to my game. And I'm always the last one without a ride at games." The tears threatened again. Jamie sniffed and hoped they'd go away.

Her mom stopped by the car and put her arms around Jamie. "I know, sweetie. It just isn't fair."

IT'S NOT FAIR

If you have a brother or sister with an ASD, you have probably thought those words before. And you are right. It isn't fair that your brother or sister has an ASD, and it isn't fair that your family has to deal with it. No matter what, understand that your feelings are normal. It's okay to get angry and to feel like things aren't fair. It's also okay to get jealous of any extra attention your sibling is getting, or to feel embarrassed about your brother's or sister's behavior in public. Everyone feels these things from time to time.

If you have a sibling with an ASD, it's important to share your feelings and ask questions.

As a sibling of someone with an ASD, you might also be experiencing positive feelings, such as pride in how far your sibling has come, or pride in yourself for being so knowledgeable about something your classmates may know nothing about. You may worry about how people will treat your sibling on the spectrum, or who will care for them when they get older. Or, you may worry about how to care for them now and still have your own life. Maybe you understand your brother or sister better than your mom and dad; this can be cool, but it can also feel like a burden.

Like any sibling relationship, you probably feel a huge mix of emotions for your brother or sister on the spectrum. Friendly or angry, proud or jealous, grateful or grumbling—you are entitled to all these feelings. ASDs are complicated. It only makes sense that your feelings about them would be complicated too.

TAKING CARE OF YOU

With all of the challenges that accompany growing up with a sibling on the spectrum, you need to remember to take care of yourself. The following are strategies that can help you reap the benefits of living with an ASD and minimize the stress that might come along with it.

TALK IT OUT WITH PARENTS

Every family is different in how they handle having a family member with an ASD. Some families discuss the topic of autism and related challenges as easily as other families discuss the weather. If your family is like this, it is probably pretty easy to talk about what you need, what you are feeling, and what might help when problems arise.

In other families, the word *autism* is barely mentioned. If your family is like this, it might take a little more work to raise your thoughts, questions, and concerns. Maybe you are mad at your mom and dad because it feels like they are always paying attention to your brother or sister. Or maybe you don't want to upset them or add to their burden by bringing up your feelings. Your feelings are important, and if you are feeling down, overburdened, or upset about something, it is important to let your parents know.

Sometimes parents think they are being helpful, but they need you to help them understand when it is not enough. For example, Jamie's mom shows that she understands her daughter's feelings, but she does not solve Jamie's problem. If fixing the situation is important to Jamie, then she needs to raise this to her mom. She might say something like, "I really appreciate your hearing me out and

TIPS FOR TALKING TO PARENTS

When going to parents to ask them for a change, here are some ideas that might lead to a more successful interaction:

- Start by acknowledging their efforts.
- Share your gratitude for what they have tried, your empathy for what they are experiencing, and then share whatever challenging feelings you might have.
- Talk about what you would like to have happen in the future and avoid focusing blame on anything that may have happened in the past.
- Be prepared to meet them in the middle. They might be able to accommodate only some of what you want.
- Remember: change comes slowly. Aim to improve the situation during each interaction rather than all at once.

understanding my feelings. But it would mean a lot to me if you could come to my games. Can we work together to find a sitter for Jack during my games? Maybe I can take care of our neighbor's child in exchange for her watching Jack." This will make it clearer to Jamie's mom that what would help is her mom actually being there. Parents cannot help you solve your problems or work out your feelings if they do not understand them.

Sharing feelings with your parents can be challenging—especially when some of the feelings you are sharing might be hard for them to hear. If you're not comfortable talking with them directly, try writing them a letter. You can also discuss your feelings with a friend before initiating a conversation with your parents.

TALK IT OUT WITH FRIENDS

It can also be helpful to talk to a friend. Being open and honest with your friends can ease any awkwardness about ASDs. It might help them treat your sibling in a way that makes you feel more comfortable. It might also help them understand you better. It will lay the groundwork for a support system when you do have a problem and need a good listener. Sometimes all you need is a good shoulder to cry on, so reaching out to your friends can go a long way toward giving you the support you need.

There are also times when you just feel like you can't share your feelings with anyone. Maybe you are too embarrassed, too angry, or just not sure what to feel. In these situations, it is still best not to keep your feelings to yourself. Your school counselor is a perfect person to share these feelings with. The counselor will keep whatever you share confidential, and he or she can help you manage your feelings or your situation.

SUPPORT GROUPS

Support groups for siblings of people with an ASD offer a chance for you to be around others who understand you in ways that even your best friends may not be able to. Not only do sibling support groups give you a safe, accepting place to talk about your experiences, but they also give you a chance to talk to people who actually

MAKE YOUR OWN CHOICES

As a sibling of an individual with a special need, you will receive tons of advice. Some people will feel you need to be more accepting, and some will accuse you of letting others walk all over you. Some will encourage you to lead your own life, and some will urge you to take responsibility for your brother or sister. You just cannot please everyone. However, be sure to keep in mind that the most important person to please is you. You are the person who will actually be in your own shoes. Do what fits you best.

"get it." Go online to research support groups in your area.

TIME FOR HELP FROM A PROFESSIONAL?

Occasionally feeling down, anxious, or upset is normal. Feeling that way constantly for a long time may be an indication you need help. Here are some signs that sadness or anxiety have gone too far:

- Feeling that you have nothing to look forward to

- Wanting to sleep more or less than usual

- Wanting to eat more or less than usual

- Avoiding activities you used to enjoy

If you have thoughts of hurting yourself in any way, get help immediately. Talk to your parents, a friend, a school counselor, or a trusted teacher if you are experiencing these warning signs. Ask them to help you get to a professional psychologist.

TAKING TIME ALONE

Finding time for yourself is just as important as connecting with others. Maybe you feel like your whole household revolves around your sibling. Maybe the chaos of living with someone with an ASD is sometimes too much to handle. Allowing

Finding some alone time to journal or do art can be an outlet for the stress of living with someone with an ASD.

yourself the space and time to rejuvenate and replenish is crucial in keeping your stress levels down. This may be something you need to speak to your parents about. Make it clear to them that you want and need this time. They can help make sure you get the alone time you need.

Once you get some alone time, consider journaling. Like talking to a friend, journaling helps you get things off your chest. You can write things to a journal that you may not feel comfortable saying to even your closest friend. You can keep your journal hidden or get a lock

IDEAS FOR ALONE TIME

- Take a hot bath.
- Look up aromatherapy ideas and incorporate them into your daily routine.
- Dance! Or do something fun to be active.
- Start a hobby—distraction can be very therapeutic!
- Make a list of all the things you are grateful for.

to give you extra confidence that no one else will read it. During alone time, you can also pursue other hobbies or interests that comfort you. Some people find that drawing, painting, or photography helps them feel more grounded or relaxed. Other people play musical instruments or go for walks. The important part of alone time is that you do something that helps *you*.

ON THE BRIGHT SIDE . . .

Though this chapter focuses on the times you need support, recognizing the unique gift of having a sibling with an ASD is important too. Many people feel lucky to have a sibling with an ASD and go on later in life to work with others who have ASDs. Siblings of people with an ASD also tend to admire their siblings more and quarrel with them less than they would siblings with no disabilities.[1] Some may feel they have more empathy and understanding toward people who are "different." Many siblings of individuals on the spectrum report they are far more skilled at teaching and managing behavior than people with neurotypical brothers and sisters. As is the case with everything in life, living with someone who has an ASD has its ups and downs, goods and bads. The important part is to recognize the good things and ask for help to work through the challenges.

ASK YOURSELF THIS

- *What sorts of feelings have you had about your brother or sister with an ASD? How do you manage feelings that may be hurtful?*

- *What are some ways you can broach a hard topic with your parents?*

- *What do you do to take care of yourself when you feel stressed out?*

- *Do you have friends who understand your situation? Do you feel they get where you're coming from?*

- *What support groups are in your area for siblings of people with an ASD?*

9

HOW CAN I HELP?
FRIENDS WITH
AN ASD

Jamie and her best friend, Marian, walked home from school with Jack. Jack mumbled to himself quietly as they walked. "Jack, why don't you tell me what's on your mind?" Marian asked. She had known Jack since he was only two. She and Jamie had become best friends in preschool, and Jack had been part of the Jamie package.

"I had a terrible day today," Jack shared, and he relayed the story of what had happened at lunch with Kerry.

"Jack, I know she hurt your feelings, but you have to remember what we talked about. How do you think things looked to her?" Marian then began to analyze the situation with Jack.

Jamie looked at her friend and smiled. She was so relieved to have someone who "got" Jack. It was a lot for Jamie to always be explaining things to him. Honestly, she felt like she ran out of patience sometimes. Having Marian be a friend to Jack was an enormous comfort. Not only did it take some of the weight off her shoulders, but she also felt good knowing Jack had someone else who was looking out for him.

HOW TO HELP

Marian has always been there for Jamie. The news that Jack had an ASD had been a shock to everyone. Marian had heard of autism before but didn't know much more than the name. In order to be a good friend, Marian knew she had to do her own research.

GET INFORMED

One of the best ways to be a supportive friend is to stay informed. Oodles of information about ASDs is available on the Internet, in books, and in the media. Everywhere you look, ASDs are making the news.

Staying informed can give you valuable insight into what your friend may be going through, whether your friend has an ASD or has a sibling with an ASD. Checking out the latest books, blogs, or news stories about ASDs can help you start a conversation with your friend. A simple Internet search should get you started. You can also ask a librarian, your other friends, or a teacher to point you in the right direction for resources. Staying informed will help you know what questions to ask, what questions not to ask, and how to be supportive of your friend.

BE AVAILABLE

Your friend living with an ASD faces some unique stressors in everyday life. He or she will need a sympathetic shoulder to cry on at times, or an ear to vent to. The best thing you can be at that time is available.

Being available does not just mean being there. It means being ready with empathy and saying "see ya" to judgments. Some of your friend's feelings may seem harsh and out of proportion to the situation. It doesn't matter that your friend's feelings make sense to you; it matters that those feelings make sense to your friend, in the context of his or her own experiences. It might be tempting to think, "If I were in her situation, I would . . ." However, we all know it's a lot easier to say you would act a certain way in a tough situation than to actually do it. If your friend shares his or her feelings with you, the best thing you can do is listen. Chances are, your friend just needs to say some of the bad feelings out loud.

LISTENING

Are you a good listener? Think about it for a second. Do you:

- Give your friend your undivided attention when she's speaking?
- Give your friend time to say what she needs to say?
- Withhold judgment?
- Let silence happen if it needs to?
- Really try to understand things from her perspective?
- Stop yourself from interrupting?
- Ask open-ended questions?
- Listen without formulating what you'll say next?
- Repeat important parts to make sure you understand what she means?
- Let her know you care?

It's easy to think that just hearing what someone has to say is actually listening. But listening is a skill that we need to learn. The next time your friend is talking to you, see if you are hitting these checkpoints. Almost everyone can benefit from working on being a good listener.

If a friend confides in you about his or her experiences either as a person with an ASD or as a sibling of someone with an ASD, keep the conversation confidential. One of the most important things you can do for this person you care about is provide a safe, nonjudgmental place for your friend to be honest about his or her feelings and experiences. Out of respect for the trust your friend has placed in you, keep the information to yourself.

WATCH FOR WARNING SIGNS

Being a good listener is just half the battle of being a good friend. Another way to help is to keep your eye out for any major changes in behavior that seem destructive. Watch for signs of depression.

If you notice your friend has stopped doing activities she used to love, or that her sleep patterns have changed, or that she talks about being worthless, it might be time to talk to her about seeking help. You can point her in the direction of helpful Web sites or books, and can encourage her to speak to a parent, guidance counselor, or teacher. Of course, if your friend says anything about feeling suicidal, tell a teacher or a parent immediately, even if your friend asks you not to. That is the one time you do not have to keep your friend's feelings private! Although you might feel like you are

You can do a lot to help make social situations less confusing and overwhelming for your friend with an ASD.

betraying your friend, you might literally be saving his or her life by going to a trusted adult.

STRUCTURE EVENTS

If your friend has an ASD, or has someone in his or her life with an ASD, events and outings can be tricky and overwhelming. One thing you can do as a friend is to structure ASD-friendly situations that are less threatening and confusing.

For instance, if your friend has problems with bright lights and loud music, you can keep the music down at your birthday party. If your friend has trouble with new people, when you invite him to hang out with a group of friends, choose friends that are familiar to him. Though you don't need to devote your life to accommodating someone else, with a little thought, you may be able to find ways to incorporate your friend into your plans and ease any potential discomfort.

BE FLEXIBLE

In the same vein as structuring events, it's important that you understand if your friend can't make it to something because of reasons related to his or her ASD. For example, Jamie will sometimes cancel plans with Marian because of

SOCIALIZING WITH YOUR FRIEND WITH AN ASD

So, you have a friend with Asperger's and maybe you want to interact usefully with him. Here are some tips:

- Prepare him for the people at a party. Let him know who is coming and what types of personalities you think might be there.
- Prepare the other people at the party to meet your friend with Asperger's so they know that if there is no hugging or eye contact, it's not personal.
- Don't tell your friend he's acting funny.
- Listen to your friend. If your friend gets overwhelmed and has to go, let him go and don't try to talk him into staying longer.

extra work she has to do to help Jack. Although Marian gets disappointed, she understands that sometimes plans just can't work out—especially with a friend who is living with an ASD.

FRIENDS ARE FRIENDS

You might want to help your friend deal with his or her ASD, but be mindful of keeping one another on equal footing. Try to be a friend, not a teacher or caregiver. Just as you might offer your friend suggestions, be sure to listen and respect suggestions offered to you as well.

DON'T FORGET YOU!

Taking care of your friend with an ASD means also taking care of yourself. It would be easy to forget about yourself and your needs in helping your friend; however, you have needs too, and you should not ignore them. If you are angry with your friend, upset, or depressed, that's normal. Your feelings are just as important as your friend's, and it does you no good to keep them bottled in. You can be compassionate and understanding while still taking care of your own needs in the situation. Don't let yourself be so immersed in helping others that you don't help yourself—you are very important!

Share your knowledge with others and be an advocate for your friend with an ASD.

SPEAK UP!

You're an advocate, a good friend, you know how to make your environment better for someone with an ASD, and you are also taking care of your own needs. The only other thing left to do is to speak up! Talk to other people about ASDs and the things you know about them. Recommend books and Web sites to your friends and loved ones. You could even get creative and make your own YouTube video or Facebook page. Letting people know about ASDs—the good, the bad, and the lovely—will help make the world a little bit better. All because of you!

ASK YOURSELF THIS

- *Do you have any friends you know or suspect might have an ASD? How can you tell?*

- *Have you told your friends about your loved one with an ASD? How do you describe the disorder?*

- *How do your other friends treat your friend with an ASD? Have you ever had to intervene?*

- *Have you ever wished you had stood up for your friend with an ASD but didn't? What would you do if put in the same situation now?*

- *What was the most difficult situation you've had to handle with your loved one who has an ASD?*

SPEAK OUT

When well-liked people speak out about their support for people with autism spectrum disorders, it sways other people's opinions. Clay Aiken is one example of an individual who used his celebrity to support people with autism spectrum disorders. He started the National Inclusion Project with Diane Bubel, a parent of a former student of his with an ASD. This project facilitates community programs that bring together typically developing children and children with disabilities such as ASDs. Programs focus on recreation opportunities, service learning, and providing funding for future programs.

10

MOVING FORWARD: LIVING WITH AN ASD

Jack's talk with Marian really opened up his eyes. With Marian's help, Jack was determined to try to talk to Kerry again. Jack's opportunity came the very next morning. He walked into the school building and found himself directly behind her. Kerry tripped and spilled all the books she had been holding. As Marian had instructed, Jack tried hard to view this interaction from Kerry's point of view. He realized she probably would like help with her books, so he bent down and helped her scoop them up.

"Thanks, Jack," Kerry smiled.

"No problem," Jack responded, and followed up with, "Hey, I am really sorry about yesterday. I should not have yelled at everyone. I hope I didn't embarrass you."

"That's okay," she responded, "I know you don't mean any harm."

It was Jack's turn to smile. He wondered what she might like now . . . "Would you like me to carry these to class for you?" he guessed.

"Sure," Kerry responded.

Jack thought this might be the best morning of his life.

MANAGING ASDs

Living with an autism spectrum disorder can be a real challenge.

ASD ROMANCE

Many people with ASDs have successful romantic relationships. There is no reason someone with an ASD cannot date or marry. Every individual has quirks that present challenges in relationships, and it is no different for individuals on the spectrum.

Professionals know little about how people develop ASDs, how each individual with an ASD will progress, and how to best treat individuals with ASDs. If experts in the field know so little, how is any teenager living with this disorder supposed to manage?

Remember that you are not alone. Thousands of other teens around the world know exactly what you are going through. Thousands more are working to make sure your voice is heard and your challenges acknowledged. Each day, scientists are researching possible treatments for ASDs. People living with an ASD are also learning that this is a different way of being, not a wrong way of being. With so many people on your side, you can look forward to a future full of opportunities and support for individuals with ASDs.

LIKE MOVIES?

Check out *I Am Sam, Mercury Rising, What's Eating Gilbert Grape?* and *Rain Man.* These movies all have characters with an ASD. Pay attention to how these characters interact with the world around them. Can you relate to their behavior?

People with ASDs can have productive lives filled with opportunities.

ASK YOURSELF THIS

- *Where do you see yourself five years from now? How will you get there?*

- *Who is the most inspiring person you know with an ASD? How does this person inspire you?*

- *What type of career do you hope to have in the future and why?*

- *What are your top five strengths? What are your top five weaknesses?*

- *What would you do if scientists discovered a cure for ASDs? Why would you respond this way?*

JUST THE FACTS

Autism is part of a larger spectrum of disorders called autism spectrum disorders. Other disorders in the spectrum include Asperger's syndrome and pervasive developmental disorder not otherwise specified.

An average of one in 110 children in the United States is diagnosed with an ASD.

Symptoms of ASDs include difficulty with social interaction, language difficulties or delays, limited interests, and repetitive behaviors. Symptoms also often include sensitivity to light, sound, and touch.

No one knows the exact cause of ASDs.

There is no known way to prevent ASDs.

There is no known "cure" for ASDs. Some people with ASDs take medications for other reasons, such as depression, or to stop obsessive behaviors.

ASDs are thought to be caused by a combination of genetic and environmental factors.

Twins studies show that if one twin has an ASD, the other twin has between a 60 and 96 percent chance of also having an ASD.

Approximately 10 percent of people with an ASD have additional disorders such as fragile X syndrome or tuberous sclerosis.

Diagnosis usually happens between the ages of three and five.

The only known effective treatment is called applied behavioral analysis (ABA).

There is no conclusive link between childhood vaccinations and ASDs.

Many people with ASDs can function normally in society and can live independently as adults. Resources for independent living, such as group homes and job coaches, are still limited.

WHERE TO TURN

If You or Someone in Your Family Might Have an ASD

First steps include getting a diagnosis and then working on an individual plan that will help with treatment. If you are overwhelmed or you need more information, you can call the National Autism Hotline: 304-525-8014. Be aware, though, that this line is not toll-free. ASDs have many symptoms and many different ways of manifesting. Finding the right diagnosis and treatment plan is crucial for those with an ASD.

If You Are Researching Treatment Options

There is a vast array of services for ASDs available throughout the nation. You can research what resources you have in your area by checking the Autism Speaks Web site: www.autismspeaks.org. Are there schools specifically for people with ASDs? Occupational therapists? Psychologists? Primary care doctors or specialists who specialize in treating people with ASDs? What does your doctor say about treatments? What are you comfortable with? Before any decisions are made, you should consult with your health-care team to make sure you get the most effective treatment.

If You Are Having Difficulty Coping

Are you overwhelmed? Angry? Hurt? Confused? These are all normal feelings to have if you or someone close to you has an ASD. The important part is to take care of yourself and to be open and honest about your feelings. If you feel signs of depression, talk to a trusted adult about what you can do. Speaking with your parents about your feelings, especially if you are feeling depressed, is very important.

If you are having suicidal thoughts, talk to an adult immediately, or call the teen suicide hotline at 1-800-274-TALK, or 1-800-SUICIDE. Take these thoughts very seriously, and be sure to talk to someone right away.

If You Have a Friend with an ASD

If you have a friend who is dealing with an ASD in some form, make sure to be available for them when they need to vent. Practice good listening skills and withhold judgment. Look for ways to make them feel more comfortable in social situations.

Also, stand up for your friend. If you feel threatened by a situation, though, run and get help. Don't put yourself or anyone else in danger. If you or your friend is being bullied, tell your principal, parent, teacher, or another adult you trust. Bullying is unacceptable and should never be tolerated.

GLOSSARY

casein
A protein found in milk and some other dairy products.

depression
A mental disorder marked by sadness, inactivity, loss of interest in usual activities, feelings of dejection and hopelessness, and some physical symptoms.

fragile X syndrome
An inherited disorder that is characterized by moderate to severe mental retardation and by a long face and large ears.

gluten
The sticky protein found in wheat and other foods and food-like products.

neurotypical
Typically developing.

occupational therapy
A therapy based on teaching skills that promote independence in everyday life despite mental or physical impairments or limitations.

phenylketonuria
An inherited disorder that usually causes severe mental retardation and seizures.

prognosis
The outlook of recovery for a disease.

spectrum
A continuous sequence or range.

stimulus
Something that rouses or incites to activity.

tuberous sclerosis
A genetic disorder of the skin and nervous system that is characterized by seizures, developmental delays, mental retardation, skin lesions, and small benign tumors forming in various organs.

ADDITIONAL RESOURCES

SELECTED BIBLIOGRAPHY

Asperger, Hans. "'Autistic Psychopathy' in Childhood." *Autism and Asperger Syndrome.* Ed. Uta Frith. Cambridge UP, 1991. 37–92. Print.

Baron-Cohen, S., A. Leslie, and Uta Frith. "Does the Autistic Child Have a Theory of Mind?" *Cognition* 21 (1985): 37–46. Print.

Elder, Jennifer. *Different Like Me: My Book of Autism Heroes.* London: Jessica Kingsley, 2005. Print.

Kanner, Leo. "Autistic Disturbances of Affective Contact." *Nervous Child* 2 (1943): 217–250. Print.

Lord, C., et al. "Autism Diagnostic Observation Schedule: A Standardized Observation of Communicative and Social Behavior." *Journal of Autism and Developmental Disorders* 19 (1989): 185–212. Print.

Rogers, S. J. "Empirically Supported Comprehensive Treatments for Young Children with Autism." *Journal of Clinical Child and Adolescent Psychology* 27.2 (1998): 168–179. Print.

Skinner, B. F. *Science and Human Behavior.* Toronto: MacMillan, 1953. Print.

FURTHER READINGS

Ariel, C. N., and R. A. Naseef. *Voices from the Spectrum: Parents, Grandparents, Siblings, People with Autism, And Professionals Share their Wisdom.* London: Jessica Kingsley, 2006. Print.

Jackson, L. *Freaks, Geeks, and Asperger Syndrome.* London: Jessica Kingsley, 2002. Print.

Robison, John Elder. *Be Different: Adventures of a Free Range Aspergian with Practical Advice for Aspergians, Misfits, Families, & Teachers.* New York: Crown Archetype, 2011. Print.

WEB LINKS

To learn more about living with autism, visit ABDO Publishing Company online at **www.abdopublishing.com**. Web sites about living with autism are featured on our Book Links page. These links are routinely monitored and updated to provide the most current information available.

SOURCE NOTES

CHAPTER 1. WHAT DOES *ASD* MEAN TO YOU? AN INTRODUCTION

1. Young Shin Kim et al. "Prevalence of Autism Spectrum Disorders in a Total Population Sample." *American Journal of Psychiatry* AiA (2011): 1–9. Web. 9 May 2011.

2. C. E. Rice et al. "Variation in the Prevalence of the Pervasive Developmental Disorders by Diagnostic Criteria." *INSAR*. International Society for Autism Research, 13 May 2011. Web. 7 Sept. 2011.

CHAPTER 2. A SPECTRUM OF SYMPTOMS: DEFINING ASDs

1. Catherine Rice. "Prevalence of Autism Spectrum Disorders—Autism and Developmental Disabilities Monitoring Network, United States, 2006." MMWR, CDC, 18 Dec. 2009. Web. 15 Dec. 2010.

2. Ibid.

3. Alice Park. "Autism Numbers Are Rising: The Question Is Why?" *Time Magazine*. Time Inc. 19 Dec. 2009. Web. 14 Dec. 2010.

4. "Autism Spectrum Disorders." Centers for Disease Control and Prevention, n.d. Web. 12 Dec. 2010.

5. Leo Kanner. "Autistic Disturbances of Affective Contact." *Nervous Child* 2 (1943): 217–250. Print.

6. American Psychiatric Association. *Diagnostic and Statistical Manual of Mental Disorders*. 4th ed. Washington, DC: APA, 2000. 71. Print.

7. Hans Asperger. "'Autistic Psychopathy' in Childhood." *Autism and Asperger Syndrome*. Ed. Uta Frith. Cambridge, 1991. 37–92. Print.

8. Ibid.

CHAPTER 3. WHY ME? CAUSES AND PREVENTION

1. C. M. Freitag. "The Genetics of Autistic Disorders and its Clinical Relevance: A Review of the Literature." *Molecular Psychiatry* 12.1 (2007): 2–22. Print.

2. K. Stromland et al. "Autism in Thalidomide Embryopathy: A Population Study." *Developmental Medicine & Child Neurology* 36.4 (1994): 351–356. Print.

3. Leo Kanner. "Autistic Disturbances of Affective Contact." *Nervous Child* 2 (1943): 217–250. Print.

4. "Learning About Autism." *genome.gov.* National Human Genome Research Institute, n.d. Web. 23 Aug. 2011.

CHAPTER 4. FIX IT! CURRENT TREATMENTS FOR ASDs

1. C. B. Ferster and B. F. Skinner. *Schedules of Reinforcement.* New York: Appleton–Century–Crofts, 1957. Print.

SOURCE NOTES CONTINUED

CHAPTER 5. WHAT ELSE MIGHT WORK? ALTERNATIVE TREATMENTS

1. Salynn Boyles. "Chelation Study for Autism Called Off." *WebMD*. WebMD, 2005–2011. Web. 7 Sept. 2011.

2. L. D. Sanders. *Discovering Research Methods in Psychology: A Student's Guide.* Malden, MA: Blackwell, 2010. 110. Print.

CHAPTER 6. WHO GETS IT: PUBLIC UNDERSTANDING AND SUPPORT

1. "Employment Research and Reports." *AutismNow.org.* The Arc of the United States, 2011. n.d. Web. 23 Aug. 2011.

2. "Adults with Autism." *Child-Autism-Parent-Cafe.com.* ASD Concepts, 2005–2011. 12 July 2011. Web. 23 Aug. 2011.

CHAPTER 7. SURVIVAL TOOLS: TEENS ON THE SPECTRUM

1. M. Mary Konstantareas. "Anxiety and Depression in Children and Adolescents with Asperger Syndrome." *Children, Youth, and Adults with Asperger Syndrome: Integrating Multiple Perspectives.* Ed. Kevin P. Stoddart. London: Jessica Kingsley, 2005. 52–55. Print.

2. "Effects of Bullying." *StopBullying.gov.* US Department of Health and Human Services, n.d. Web. 31 Jan. 2011.

CHAPTER 8. LEARNING TO COPE: SIBLINGS WITH AN ASD

1. Laura Kaminsky and Deborah Dewey. "Siblings Relationships of Children with Autism." *Journal of Autism and Developmental Disorders* 31.4 (2001): 399–410. Print.

CHAPTER 9. HOW CAN I HELP? FRIENDS WITH AN ASD

None.

CHAPTER 10. MOVING FORWARD: LIVING WITH AN ASD

None.

INDEX

ABOUT THE AUTHOR

Megan Atwood is a freelance writer and editor working in the Twin Cities. She also teaches creative writing classes and other college courses for a variety of places around the metro area.

PHOTO CREDITS